Big Talkabout Cards
Stages 1–4
Roderick Hunt

Teaching Notes

Contents

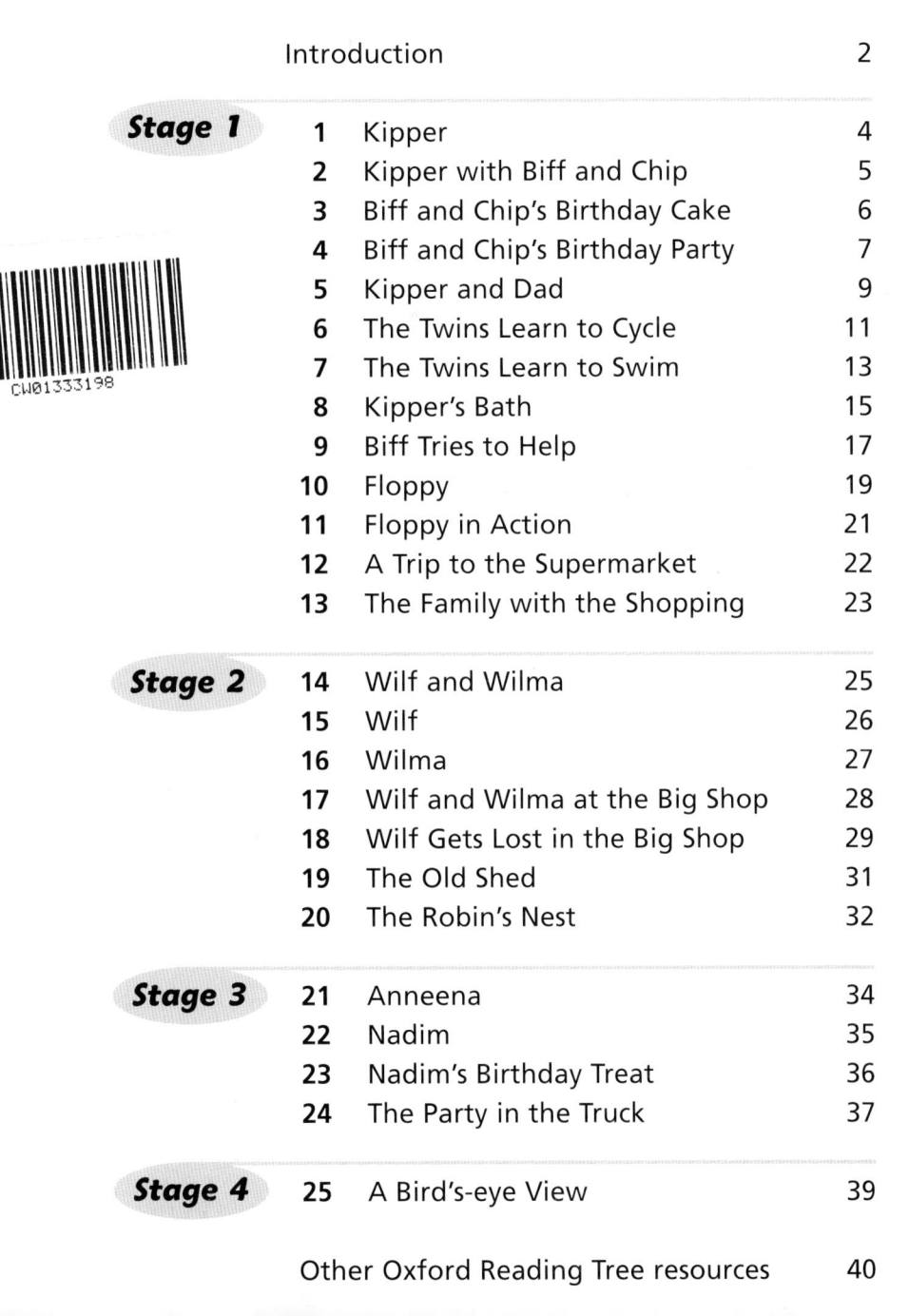

		Introduction	2
Stage 1	1	Kipper	4
	2	Kipper with Biff and Chip	5
	3	Biff and Chip's Birthday Cake	6
	4	Biff and Chip's Birthday Party	7
	5	Kipper and Dad	9
	6	The Twins Learn to Cycle	11
	7	The Twins Learn to Swim	13
	8	Kipper's Bath	15
	9	Biff Tries to Help	17
	10	Floppy	19
	11	Floppy in Action	21
	12	A Trip to the Supermarket	22
	13	The Family with the Shopping	23
Stage 2	14	Wilf and Wilma	25
	15	Wilf	26
	16	Wilma	27
	17	Wilf and Wilma at the Big Shop	28
	18	Wilf Gets Lost in the Big Shop	29
	19	The Old Shed	31
	20	The Robin's Nest	32
Stage 3	21	Anneena	34
	22	Nadim	35
	23	Nadim's Birthday Treat	36
	24	The Party in the Truck	37
Stage 4	25	A Bird's-eye View	39
		Other Oxford Reading Tree resources	40

Introduction

The Big Talkabout Cards are children's first introduction to the characters and settings in the Oxford Reading Tree stories. By using the Big Talkabout Cards children will learn the names of the characters, and then learn to read the characters' names and the first key words. The cards concentrate on developing the early recognition skills that children need to become competent readers.

This Teaching Notes booklet provides:
- background information on each character
- an exciting story to accompany each card
- stimulating questions to encourage discussion
- cross-curricular links.

The cards and accompanying stories have been illustrated to encourage conversation. Children will have often have had experiences that compare with the situations in the illustrations and the stories. The questions at the end of each story are designed to familiarise the children with the main characters, encourage them to share their experiences with each other, and help them to identify with the characters and their feelings. This will give the children confidence and encourage them to express themselves more readily in conversation.

The Big Talkabout Cards

Each card is bordered with the relevant Oxford Reading Tree stage colour.

Stage 1 (grey)
Big Talkabout Cards 1–13 introduce Kipper, Biff and Chip, Mum and Dad and Floppy

Stage 2 (green)
Big Talkabout Cards 14–20 introduce Wilf and Wilma

Stage 3 (blue)
Big Talkabout Cards 21–24 introduce Anneena and Nadim

Stage 4 (red)
Big Talkabout Card 25 introduces the neighbourhood where all the Oxford Reading Tree children live. It is a visual guide to the places

which feature in many of the stories, and it acts as a link between the earlier Stages 1-3 stories and those of Stage 4 upwards. At later stages, this card can provide the opportunity for the children to revisit the neighbourhood to recall various incidents and adventures.

The Teaching Notes

Use the following headings in the Teaching Notes to help you to introduce each card.

Before reading
Show the card to the children. Look at the picture together and talk about what you can see. Write the character's name/s in the space provided above the picture, together with any other words of interest.

Read to the children
Read the short background notes on each character. Then read the story to the children.

Ask the children
Finally use the question prompts to encourage the children to talk about the character/s and the situations depicted in the picture.

Cross-curricular links
These provide links to different curricular areas, with questions to fulfil suggested objectives.

Stage 1

1 Kipper

Before reading

Show Card 1 to the children. Talk about the little boy (**Kipper**) and write his name in the space at the top of the card.

Read to the children

This is Kipper. Kipper is four years old. Kipper sometimes gets into trouble. His real name is not Kipper, it's Christopher, but when he was very little and learning to talk, he used to say Kipper, which sounds a bit like Christopher. His Dad said to him, "I don't know why we called you Christopher when you can't even say it properly. Anyway I think Kipper suits you."

So from then on, everyone called him Kipper.

Ask the children

- Do you remember what Kipper's real name is?
- What sort of boy do you think Kipper is?
- Do you think he is always good, or is he sometimes naughty?
- What are some of Kipper's favourite toys?
- What are your favourite toys? What toy do you like to have in bed?
- Does anyone have a special name for you? Is it funny?
- Can you think of other ways that people shorten names (Bobby for Robert, Sue for Susan, Katie for Katherine etc).

Cross-curricular links

Knowledge & understanding of the world: identify features of living things.
Science: look at similarities/differences/patterns

- How does Kipper look the same as you?
- How does he look different to you?

2 Kipper with Biff and Chip

Before reading
Show Card 2 to the children. Talk about the two children and write the names **Biff** and **Chip** at the top of the card.

Read to the children
This is a picture of Kipper with his sister Biff, and his brother Chip. Biff and Chip are older than Kipper and there is something special about them. They are twins.

Kipper likes having an older brother and sister. Biff and Chip like having Kipper for their little brother - although sometimes he can make a lot of fuss when he doesn't want to do something. Some twins look exactly alike, but the twins that look like each other are always either boy twins, or girl twins. Biff and Chip look similar, but because they are a boy and a girl they are not exactly the same.

Ask the children
- Do you know any twins? What are their names?
- Are they identical?

Cross-curricular links
Personal, social and emotional development: develop respect for cultures and beliefs
PSHE: develop awareness of their own and other people's needs
- How is your family different to Kipper's family?
- What makes your family different to your friends' families?

3 Biff and Chip's Birthday Cake

Before reading
Show Card 3 to the children. Write the names **Biff** and **Chip** at the top of the card.

📖 Read to the children
This is a story about how Biff and Chip got their names.

Biff's real name is not Biff. It's Barbara. Chip's real name is not Chip. It's David. But when Kipper was little he couldn't say Barbara. He said Biff. And he couldn't say David. He said Chip. Biff and Chip don't sound a bit like Barbara and David, but that's how Kipper said it and it made everyone laugh.

One day the twins' mother was making them a birthday cake for their seventh birthday. She said, "I'm not very good at putting names on a birthday cake and Barbara and David are very long names to write in icing sugar. So I'm going to put Biff and Chip instead." And she did!

"It's funny being twins," said Biff. "Our friends have to bring two presents – one for each of us."

"Which one of us was born first?" said Chip.

"Mum!" Called Biff. "Am I older than Chip or is Chip older than me? Which one of us was born first?"

"I'm not going to say," said Mum. "If I told you, one of you might start getting bossy!"

💬 Ask the children
- How old are Biff and Chip? How many candles are on their cake?
- Do you have an older brother or sister, or a younger brother or sister?
- What do you think it would it be like to be a twin? Would you like to be one?

◀▶ Cross-curricular link
Maths: count reliably up to 10 everyday objects
- How many candles are on Biff and Chips cake and how many will be on their next?
- How many candles will be on your next birthday cake?

Stage 1

4 Biff and Chip's Birthday Party

Before reading
Show Card 4 to the children. Write the names **Wilf**, **Wilma**, **Anneena** and **Nadim** at the top of the card, and point each of them out to the children. Talk about party food, games and party bags. Discuss what usually happens when the cake is brought in with the candles lit.

 ### Read to the children

Biff and Chip are sitting with their friends Wilf, Wilma, Anneena and Nadim. We will read more stories about Biff and Chip's friends later on. Here is a story about Biff and Chip's seventh birthday party.

"Come and help me to set the table for your birthday party," said Mum. We have to put the food on plates and then set the table. Make sure you wash your hands first."

So Biff and Chip helped get the food ready. There were little sandwiches and chicken satays and baby sausages on sticks. There were cheesesticks, breadsticks, little pieces of celery, apples and cucumber with all sorts of tasty things to dip them in. There were little cakes and jellies. In the kitchen was the birthday cake Mum had made with seven candles on top.

There was a knock at the door. Some of Biff and Chip's friends had come. They all had two presents – one for Biff and one for Chip. Then some more friends came and Biff and Chip were soon busy opening more parcels.

"Where's Kipper?" asked Biff. "I haven't seen him for ages."

Kipper came out of the room where they had set out the food. He was covered in crumbs and he had tomato sauce all down his front!

Do you know what Kipper had done? He just couldn't wait for the time when everyone sat down to eat. So he had gone ahead and eaten his party food all by himself.

Biff looked cross with Kipper, but Chip said, "Never mind. At least he didn't try and cut himself a piece of our birthday cake."

Stage 1

"Why don't we eat now, anyway?" said Biff.
So that's what they did.
And as for Kipper, he sat down with the others and started all over again.

Ask the children

- Have you ever had a birthday party? What did you have to eat?
- Have you ever been to a birthday party? Tell me about it.
- What did Kipper do? Do you think he was naughty?
- Who has had a birthday not very long ago? Who has one soon?

Cross-curricular link

Maths: begin to use the vocabulary involved in adding and subtracting
- How many presents did Biff and Chip have for their birthday?
- How many plates, cups and forks would they need to set the table for the party?

5 Kipper and Dad

Before reading
Show Card 5 to the children. Write **Kipper** and **Dad** in the space above the picture.

Ask the children
- Do you remember Kipper?
- What do you remember about him?
- What is Dad wearing? What is Kipper wearing?
- Why do you think they are wearing these clothes?
- Do you know where Dad and Kipper are?

Read to the children

One day when Kipper was out with Dad he saw an orange concrete mixer and he said, "Look at that conkink", instead of "concrete mixer".

Then he saw a big yellow bulldozer. But he didn't say "bulldozer". Instead, he called it an "ogle-boze". "Look at that ogle-boze," he said.

Then Kipper saw some squirrels. He didn't call them squirrels. He called them giddalls. He said, "Look at all those giddalls."

His Dad said, "They're not called giddalls, they're called squirrels, Kipper."

"No they're not, they're called giddalls," said Kipper.
"Kipper, they're called squirrels," said his Dad.
"They're giddalls," said Kipper.
"They're squirrels," said Dad loudly.
"They're giddalls!"
"Squirrels!"
"Giddalls!"
"Squirrels!" yelled Dad at the top of his voice.
One of the squirrels ran to the top of the tree.
"Ssh!" said Kipper to his Dad. "You're frightening the giddalls!"

Stage 1

Ask the children
- Kipper called the bulldozer an "ogle-boze". Can you think of a funny name for some other things - like helicopter, mouse, etc.

Cross-curricular links
Knowledge & understanding of the world: observe and identify features of living things
Numeracy: know the days of the week and the seasons of the year
- What time of the year do you think it is in the picture?
- What are the clues that tell us it is this season?

6 The Twins Learn to Cycle

Before reading
Show Card 6 to the children. Write the names **Biff** and **Chip** at the top of the card and ask the children what they can remember about the twins.

Read to the children
Do you remember that Biff and Chip are twins and because they are a boy and a girl they don't look exactly alike? Can you still tell that they are twins? Do you know that lots of twins like doing things together, and they like wearing the same sort of clothes. This is what Biff and Chip think about being twins.

"We like being twins," said Biff and Chip.
Biff and Chip aren't always good friends. Sometimes they quarrel. They even fight with each other.
When they quarrel or fight, either their Mum or their Dad will say, "All right, who started it?"
And Chip will say, "She did!"
And Biff will say, "He did!"
When this happens the only thing to do is to put Biff in one room and Chip in another. Then, after a little while, they're good friends again.

Ask the children
- Do you ever quarrel? Do you ever fight? What happens in the end?
- What do you think it's like for a mum and dad to have twins? Is it easier to have one baby at a time?
- Why do you think Biff and Chip quarrel and fall out? What might they fight about?
- Why do you think people quarrel with each other?

Stage 1   11

Read to the children

Do you know what is hard about being a twin? It's when the other twin does something first, like learning to tie up shoe laces, or writing his or her name. Although it was Biff who learnt to swim before Chip, it was Chip who learned to ride a bicycle before Biff! Here is a story about how it happened.

Dad and Mum helped Biff and Chip learn to ride but Biff was a little bit frightened and Mum had to keep hold of the saddle.
  "Come on, Biff," Chip would shout. "Use the pedals, or you'll never ride your bike."
  Then one day Mum forgot to hold the saddle and Biff pedalled forward all by herself. And she found that it wasn't as difficult and frightening as she thought. Very soon she could ride her bicycle just as well as Chip could ride his.

Ask the children

- Can you ride a bike, or are you just learning to ride one? Why should we always be careful with bicycles? Why should you just ride your bike in the park or garden?
- How did you feel the first time no-one was holding your saddle and were you riding your bike all by yourself?
- Have you ever fallen off your bike?

Cross-curricular link

Maths: use everyday words to describe position and solve practical problems
- If Chip learnt to ride his bike first, who learnt to ride their bike second?
- Who do you think will learn to ride their bike third?
- How many of you came to school today on your bikes? Let's draw a pictogram of different ways you came to school.

7 The Twins Learn to Swim

Before reading

Show Card 7 to the children. Write **Biff** and **Chip** at the pool at the top of the card.

Read to the children

Here is a story about how Biff learnt to swim before Chip.

Every week Biff and Chip went to the swimming pool with their mum and dad. Biff loved the water. She liked to splash about, and she didn't mind a bit if she got her hair wet or if some of the water splashed in her face.

Chip didn't like the pool as much as Biff. He wasn't happy when the water splashed in his face. It made his eyes sting and he felt a bit frightened in case he went under the water.

Biff soon learned to swim, but it was a job to get Chip into the water at all.

"Come on in, Chip," Biff would shout, "or you'll never learn to swim."

Then one day, when Chip was in the pool and he wasn't expecting it, someone pushed into him and knocked him over. He went right under the water.

And Chip found that going under the water wasn't so bad after all. So, of course, as soon as he didn't mind getting water on his face, and wasn't frightened of going under, he very soon learned to swim just like Biff.

Ask the children

- What part of the swimming pool is dangerous? Why should we always be careful in pools and near water.
- Do you like going to the pool?

Stage 1

- Do you have swimming lessons at the pool?
- How do you feel when you do something new, something that is difficult or something that makes you nervous.

◀▶ **Cross-curricular link**

Knowledge & understanding of the world: identify features in the local area
- Where is the nearest pool to our school?
- Where else do you go swimming?

8 Kipper's Bath

Before reading

Show Card 8 and write **Kipper** at the top of the card.

 Read to the children

Here is the story of one of Kipper's bathtimes.

Kipper was having a great time in the bath one night. It was all because he'd taken an empty washing-up liquid bottle with him to the bathroom.

He filled the washing-up bottle with water and when he squeezed it the water came squirting out in a thin jet. "This is good," said Kipper to himself. He splashed water against the side of the bath. He whooshed it up in the air like a fountain. Best of all he liked shooting water at his feet, trying to hit one toe at a time.

"I hope you're not getting water all over the bathroom floor," called Kipper's dad. "Make sure you wash yourself all over with the soap and flannel. I'll be up in a minute to get you out and help you dry yourself."

Kipper washed himself all over. Then he pulled the plug out to let the water run away. The water went round very fast and things began to get sucked down to the plug hole with a noise that sounds a bit like this – ssschloop!

Kipper had a little plastic cowboy in the bath. He watched it float towards the whirlpool over the plug hole. It went round and round in smaller and smaller circles and then - ssschloop! Down it went.

Now Kipper did something very silly. He tried to get the cowboy from the bottom of the whirlpool. And ssschloop! His hand was sucked into the little round grille inside the plug hole.

"Ouch!" said Kipper. And when he tried to pull his hand out, he couldn't. His finger was stuck. However hard he tugged, he couldn't get his finger out.

Stage 1

"Help!" he yelled. "My finger's stuck in the plug hole."

Kipper's dad came rushing into the bathroom. "I don't know," he said. "This is what happens when I leave you to have a bath by yourself."

Dad tried to pull Kipper's finger out but it was stuck fast.

"Ow! Ooh! Ouch! You're hurting," cried Kipper.

Chip came into the bathroom to see what was happening. "You may have to call the fire brigade," he said to Dad.

"I don't want firemen to come," wailed Kipper. "I haven't got any clothes on."

Biff came into the bathroom to see what all the noise was about.

"Kipper's got his finger stuck down the plug hole," Chip told her.

Biff said that she would try and help Kipper.

◀▶ Cross-curricular links

PSHE: manage own personal hygiene
Knowledge and understanding of the world: ask questions about how things happen
- Why is Kipper having a bath?
- What would happen if you didn't have a bath?
- How else do we keep ourselves clean and healthy?
- How did Kipper's fingers get stuck?

9 Biff Tries to Help

Before reading

Show Card 9 to the children and write **Kipper**, **Biff** and **Chip** in the space at the top of the card. Then continue the story.

Read to the children

Biff pulled Kipper's finger but he yelled even louder.
"Ouch!" yelled Kipper. "You're worse than Dad."
Just then Mum came back.
"Whatever's going on," she gasped. "The minute I leave you by yourselves there's trouble."
"Get my finger out," sniffed Kipper.
"All right, now just hold still," said Mum. She got some washing-up liquid and squeezed some on to Kipper's finger. Then she gently pulled the finger out of the plug hole. "I don't know," said Mum. "All it takes is a little common sense. I just hope that nothing else has gone wrong while I've been out."
She helped Kipper out of the bath and stepped back on the toothpaste tube that Kipper had left lying on the floor.
The toothpaste squirted all over the carpet. I wouldn't like to tell you what Mum had to say after that!

Ask the children

- What sort of toys do you have in the bath?
- Have you ever watched the water go down the plug hole?
- How did Mum get Kipper's finger free? Why did she use washing-up liquid?
- How do you think Kipper felt when his finger was stuck. Was he upset or frightened?
- How do you feel when you get into difficulties or hurt yourself?

Read to the children

Kipper has written this song to sing at bathtime. We can do the actions together.

Stage 1

Song at Bath Time by Kipper
There's the towel,
the soap is in the dish, dish, dish.
Here's the water running
with a swish, swish, swish.
(Stroke hands backwards and forwards)

The foam is white and frothy,
smooth it flat, flat, flat.
Squish the soap all over
with a split, splat, splat.
(Slap thighs gently with palms of hands)

Watch the water curling
down the plug, plug, plug.
Listen to it gurgling
with a glug, glug, glug.
(Flip bottom lip downwards with index finger)

◀▶ **Cross-curricular link**

Knowledge and understanding of the world: Ask questions about why things happen and how things work
- Why was Mum going to call the fire brigade?
- What else do the fire brigade do?
- Who else helps us and what are their jobs?

10 Floppy

Before reading
Show Card 10 to the children. Write **Floppy** in the space at the top of the card.

Read to the children

Here is a story about Floppy got his name.

What sort of dog do you think this is? Is he a fierce dog? Is he a snappy, quick-tempered dog? Is he a very, very good dog who always does what he's told? No – he's none of these things. He's just a great big stupid, soppy dog who loves to romp and roll and run all over the place. He likes nothing better than to play with a stick or a ball. He loves to roll on his back to have his tummy scratched. He loves to dig holes with his big paws, or to go for a swim in the pond.

This dog belongs to Biff, Chip, and Kipper. You can read a story later on all about how the children came to own him.

What do you think this dog is called? Is he called Killer? Is he called Tiny? How about Snuffles, or Spot? How about Judy? How about Rex?

When Biff, Chip, and Kipper first had this dog, they didn't know what to call him.

In fact the children's dad called the dog "A nuisance!" This was because the dog was racing round and round the house. It chased round all the rooms, it bounded in and out of doors, it rushed up and down stairs. Then it charged into the kitchen, skidded on the mat, and knocked over a bottle of milk that was standing on the floor.

The milk spilt all over the floor, and that's when their dad called the dog a nuisance.

"I hope we haven't made a mistake," said Mum when the dog began chasing all over the house again. "Maybe we should have got a dog that is smaller and quieter."

Stage 1

"What shall we call the dog, then?" asked Kipper. "I think we should call him Marmalade Mackintosh."

"Marmalade Mackintosh! Marmalade Mackintosh!" said Biff. "What sort of a name is that? I think his name should be short. I think we should call him Prince."

"He doesn't look much like a Prince to me," said Chip. "How about Hector? That really suits him."

"It's better than Marmalade Mackintosh, at any rate," said Dad. "By the way, where is the dog? What's he up to? Why isn't he chasing all over the house?"

"He's here," said Kipper, looking under the table. "He's flopped down under the table, and he's fast asleep."

"He must have worn himself out," said Mum. "Fancy being able to flop down just like that, and fall asleep."

"Look at him," said Biff. "He's a lovely dog, really. Look at his floppy old ears."

"He's just a floppy sort of dog altogether," said Dad.

"I like that as a name," said Biff. "Floppy. That would be a good name for him."

Everyone liked the name Floppy. It suited the dog. So that's what they called him – Floppy.

Ask the children

- What did the new dog do when it first came to live with Biff, Chip, and Kipper?
- Why did Dad call it a nuisance?
- What did they call the dog in the end? Why do you think they chose that name?
- Do any of you have pets? What sort of pets do you have?
- Why do you think it is fun to have a pet?
- Why is it important to look after your pets properly? Do you know what sort of things you should do care for a pet.

Cross-curricular links

Knowledge & understanding of the world / Science: find out about and identify some features of living things, objects and events
- What dangers can you see in the picture?
- Why are these things dangerous?
- What can you see that uses electricity?

11   Floppy in Action

Before reading
Show Card 11 to the children. Talk about Floppy and write **Floppy** at the top of the card. Chip and Kipper have both written poems about Floppy. Read them to the children and ask them to suggest some action words to write above the picture.

 ### Read to the children

Chip wrote this poem:

Floppy by Chip
Our dog's a soppy dog,
a silly dog, a floppy dog.
Our dog's a lazy dog,
a chasing, racing, crazy dog.
Our dog's a happy dog,
not a mean or snappy dog.
Our dog's a wise dog,
a "look in your eyes" dog.
Our dog's a grand dog,
a loving, "lick your hand" dog.
Our dog's a true dog,
he'll always play with you, dog.
Our dog is our dog,
a full of grins and smiles dog.
You'd have to go for miles and miles,
to find a dog like our dog.

And Kipper wrote this poem:

My Dog's Bark by Kipper
(The children can all join in at the end.)
Cats go miaooow,
And cows go moooo,
Owls in trees go t'whit - t'whooooo.
My dog's bark is loud and gruff.
The noise he makes is **wruff, wruff, wruff**.

◀▶ Cross-curricular link

Communication, language and literacy: recognise, explore and work with rhyming patterns / generate new and invented words
- What were the words rhyming in Kipper's poem?
- Lets make a list of other words that rhyme with 'wruff' and 'moo'.

Stage 1   21

12 A Trip to the Supermarket

Before reading

Show Card 12 to the children and ask them to tell you who the characters are. Write **Mum** and **Dad** at the top of the card. Talk about the picture. Discuss going to the supermarket or foodstore. Ask if have any of the children have ever pushed a supermarket trolley?

Ask the children

- Which of the children do you think looks most like Mum, and which looks most like Dad?
- What is there about Chip that makes him look the most like Dad?
- What is there about Kipper that makes him look the most like Mum?
- What colour is Mum's and Kipper's hair?
- What colour is Dad's and Biff's and Chip's hair?
- What do you think that Mum is saying to Biff and Chip in this picture?

Read to the children

One day, Biff, Chip, and Kipper went to the supermarket with their mum and dad. The first thing they did was to go to the place where all the trolleys were kept.

"I want to push the trolley today," said Chip.

"That's not fair," said Biff. "I want to push the trolley. Why should Chip have it?"

"Don't argue, you two," said Mum. "You can both push a trolley. Dad's going to do one lot of shopping, and I'm going to do another. So we're not going round together. Biff can go with Dad, and Chip and Kipper can come with me."

"I hope we're going to get the fruit and vegetables," said Biff, as she and Dad set off. She loved helping to choose things like apples and tomatoes and bananas.

Mum took Chip and Kipper to get things like coffee, and sugar, and cans of soup, and beans and spaghetti.

Chip was good at helping Mum. If Mum said, "I want four cans of alphabet spaghetti," or "I want two blackcurrant jellies," Chip was able to go and get them and put them in the trolley.

Stage 1

Soon the trolley began to fill up with cans, and packets, and bags and bottles and jars.

Mum had some trouble with Kipper when it came to choosing some cereal. Kipper didn't want cornflakes, or ordinary cereal. He wanted special sorts.

"These special packets are so expensive," said Mum. "You'll just have to put up with cornflakes and shredded wheat. Maybe I'll buy something special next time, if you're good."

◀▶ **Cross-curricular link**

Mathematical development: use language (cube, cone, sphere) to describe size and shape
- What shapes can you see on the shelves in the supermarket?
- Which package is the biggest package? Which package is the smallest?
- Which one do you think is the heaviest/lightest?

13 The Family with the Shopping

Before reading

Show Card 13 to the children. Ask the children what they think could be in the cans, packets, bags and bottles. Then continue the story.

Read to the children

Very soon the shopping trolley was full. It was very heavy to push and Chip found it difficult to manage because it wouldn't go straight. It kept going sideways and it banged into the shelves, or other people's trolleys.

At last the shopping was done and they joined Biff and Dad at the checkout.

As Mum began to unload her trolley, she said, "That's funny, I didn't have this on my shopping list, or this, or this, or this. What's been going on?"

Stage 1

Among Mum's shopping was a jar of pickled onions, a tin of black treacle, a box of cake cases, a pair of large rubber gloves, some cocktail sticks, and a packet of cherries.

Everyone looked at Kipper, and Dad said, "Have you been putting things in Mum's trolley when she wasn't looking, Kipper?"

Kipper had to say that he had, and that he was only trying to help. Big tears came into his eyes when Dad looked cross and said that they'd have to put all the things back on the shelves. But he felt better when Mum said, "Well, I suppose we could make some little cakes in the cake cases."

"And we could put a cherry on top of each one," said Biff.

Dad said, "I suppose I could do with a pair of rubber gloves. They're always useful."

And Chip said, "Couldn't we keep the onions? Dad loves to eat them with cheese."

So in the end all they had to put back was the jar of black treacle and the cocktail sticks.

When they got outside Kipper said, "Did we remember to get some dog food for Floppy?"

"I didn't get any," said Mum.

"I didn't get any, either," said Dad.

So Dad had to go back and get some food for Floppy. It took Dad quite a long time to go round again, but everyone was pleased with Kipper for remembering to buy food for the dog.

Ask the children

- Do you help to push the trolley? Do you help by finding things on the shelves?
- Biff liked choosing vegetables and fruit. What do you like helping to choose?
- Can you remember going to the supermarket when you were very little? Did your mum and dad ever get cross with you?
- Do you know what is meant by cereals, vegetables, bakery, dairy produce, etc?
- What other kind of things can you buy in a supermarket apart from food?

◂▸ Cross-curricular link

Communication, language and literacy: make simple lists for planning and reminding

- What could Mum and Dad have done to help them remember their shopping?
- Let's write a list of things they needed to buy.

Stage 2

14 Wilf and Wilma

Before reading
Show Card 15 to the children and write **Wilf** and **Wilma** at the top of the card.

Read to the children
Do you have a special friend, or even two special friends? Biff and Chip do. Here they are. They are called Wilf and Wilma. They are not twins like Biff and Chip. They are just brother and sister.

Wilf and Wilma live in the same street as Biff and Chip. They live two doors away, so it is easy for them to play together after school or in the holidays.

Sometimes Wilf and Wilma's mum or dad come to Biff and Chip's house to look after them when Biff and Chip's mum and dad go out. And sometimes Biff and Chip's mum or dad go round to Wilf and Wilma's house to look after Wilf and Wilma.

Ask the children
- What are Wilf and Wilma doing in the picture?
- Who is your special friend? Where does your friend live? Do they live nearby to you?
- Do you have any brothers or a sisters, or a half-brother or half-sister?
- Do all your family get on well or do you argue sometimes?
- Does your family have another family that they are friendly with?

◀▶ Cross-curricular link
Science: recognise that plants are living and need water and light
- What can you see next to the bush in the garden?
- What do you need a watering can for?
- What else do plants need?

15 Wilf

Before reading
Show Card 15 to the children and write the name **Wilf** at the top of the card.

Read to the children
Wilf is the same age as Biff and Chip, and he is in the same class at school. Wilf likes to play football. Wilf loves his bicycle too. He loves it so much that his mum once said to him, "I'm surprised you don't take that bike to bed with you."

Ask the children
- Do you have something that you love, like Wilf loves his bike?
- Does your mum ever tease you, like Wilf's mum teases him?
- What else does Wilf like? Do you think he is good at football?

Cross-curricular link
Knowledge & understanding of the world: investigate objects and materials
- What is Wilf doing with the ball?
- Why does the ball bounce?
- What else can you find that bounces like the ball?

16 Wilma

Before reading
Show Card 16 to the children and write **Wilma** at the top of the card.

Read to the children
Wilma is a year older than Biff, Chip, and Wilf. She is in a class above them at school. Biff and Chip like playing with Wilma because she is good at thinking up new games and she always knows what to do.

Wilma is good at music. She can play the recorder and she is learning the guitar. Wilma thinks she would like to be a musician when she grows up.

Ask the children
- What are you good at like Wilma is good at music?
- Wilma wants to be a musician when she grows up. What do you want to be?
- Why do you think Biff and Chip like Wilma?

Cross-curricular link
Creative development: sing simple songs from memory
- What songs do you think Wilma might be playing?
- What other instruments could she play?

17 Wilf and Wilma at the Big Shop

Before reading

Show Card 17 to the children and write **Wilf** and **Wilma** at the top of the card. Ask if the children have ever been shopping with their mum or dad in a great big shop? Have they ever been in one of those shops with big lifts and moving staircases?

Read to the children

This is a story about what happened to Wilf when he went with his mum and Wilma to one of those big shops.

Wilma said, "I don't like shopping in these big shops. There are so many people around, and Mum always takes ages to buy anything."

"I know," said Wilf. "Who wants to look at things like ladies' dresses? Mum once spent ages looking at blouses and skirts and she ended up not buying anything at all!"

Wilf's mum had just spent ages in the kitchen department but she had only bought a new frying pan. "Please can you carry this big box for me Wilf, and don't start moaning," his mum said, "we're going to look round the toy department now. You can get some ideas about what you want for Christmas. Come on."

Wilf saw a man with a small crowd round him. The man was showing a little machine that peeled carrots and potatoes.

Wilf watched the man for a few minutes. It was amazing how quickly the machine could peel a carrot. "That would make an ideal present for Mum and Dad," he thought.

◀▶ Cross-curricular link

Communication, language and literacy: to read and use captions / labels
- What kind of writing can you see around the store?
- What is this writing called?
- What do you think the sign behind Wilf's mum says?
- What do you think the sign between the escalator says?

18 Wilf Gets Lost in the Big Shop

Before reading
Show Card 18 to the children and ask them why they think Wilf is crying. Then continue the story.

Read to the children

Wilf looked round to tell Wilma, but he couldn't see where she was. Come to that, he couldn't see Mum either. He pushed his way to the place where he had last seen them. There was no sign of them. There were just lots and lots of other people pushing and shoving past him.

Where did Mum say they were going to go next? It was to the toy department. "Perhaps that's where I'd better go," thought Wilf to himself. "I wonder how I get there?"

(Now if you are ever lost in a very busy or crowded place, don't do what Wilf did and wander off and try to find your mum or dad. The best thing to do is to stay where you are and let your mum or dad find you. And, of course, if you wait patiently, they will find you. Don't do what Wilf did!)

Wilf managed to find his way to a big staircase. There was a sign saying "Second floor – Toy Department", and so Wilf went up the stairs to the next floor and tried to find the toys, but he couldn't find them.

In the end, there seemed to be so many legs and bags and boxes and baskets to push through that Wilf began to cry. He just couldn't help it.

A lady asked Wilf if he was lost, and Wilf told her that he was. "Children sometimes do get lost in busy shops," said the lady, "so I think the best thing for me to do is to take you to the Manager's office, and then your mum will be sure to find you."

The Manager was a very kind lady. She told Wilf to wait quietly and gave him some plastic blocks to play with. "Plastic blocks are for children of Kipper's age," thought Wilf miserably, "but if I don't play with them, it might upset the kind lady."

Stage 2

At last Wilf's mum came to the office to get him. She spoke in a cheerful way to the Manager, but Wilf could tell that she was really rather cross with him.

Later, Wilma said, "Don't be cross with Wilf. Didn't you ever get lost when you were a little girl?"

"Yes, I suppose I did," said her mum. "It was a very nasty thing to happen."

"There you are then," said Wilma. "By the way, Wilf, where's that box that mum gave you to carry."

"Oh no!" said Wilf. "I left it in the Manager's office."

I won't tell you what Wilf's mum said to him after that!

Ask the children

- How did Wilf get lost? What was he looking at while Wilma and his mum went on without him?
- Was Wilf's mum cross with him at the end of the story?
- Have you ever been lost? What did it feel like? How soon were you found again?
- Why is it better to stay where you are if you ever get lost in a busy place?

Cross-curricular link

Communication, language & literacy: use talk to organise ideas, feelings and events
- What do you think Wilf is saying to the lady?
- Why do you think the lady approached Wilf?

19 The Old Shed

Before reading

Show Card 19 to the children and write **Wilma** and **Dad** at the top of the card. Look at the picture and talk about what you see. Then tell this story.

Read to the children

"I must mend the old shed," said Wilma's dad. "I've been meaning to patch it up for ages and ages, but I just haven't had the time to get round to it."

Wilma looked at her dad. "What the shed needs is a new roof, new walls, a new floor, a new window, and a new door," she said.

"Don't be so cheeky," laughed Wilma's dad. "All it needs is a few bits of wood here and there. In fact I'll go and mend it now and you can come and help me."

So Wilma went with her dad to the old shed that stood at the end of the garden.

"You're quite right, Wilma," said her dad as he unlocked the door. "Maybe I do need a new shed after all."

In fact, the old shed had almost fallen down. There was a hole in the roof, the window was broken and all the wood on one side was rotten.

Wilma and her dad peered inside the shed as the old door creaked open.

"Oh!" gasped Wilma in surprise. "Just look at that!"

There, in the corner of the shed was an old sheet that Wilma's dad had used to cover up the lawn-mower. Right on top of the sheet was a perfectly round bird's nest. When they looked, Wilma and her dad saw that inside the nest were five small white eggs with brown speckles on them.

Ask the children

- Is Wilma right, does her dad need a new shed? What is wrong with the old one?
- Why were Wilma and her dad surprised? What was in the shed?

Stage 2

◀▶ **Cross-curricular links**

Knowledge & understanding of the world / Science: make observations of common objects and communicate these
- What materials would Wilma's Dad need to mend the shed?
- What would be a good material to have for the roof?

20 The Robin's Nest

Before reading

Show Card 20 to the children. Look at the picture and talk about what you see. Write a list at the top of the card, e.g. **nest**, **eggs**, **rake**. Then continue the story.

 Read to the children

Very gently, Wilma's dad felt the eggs with the back of his fingers. "It's a robin's nest, Wilma," he said, "and the eggs are still warm. That means the robins will soon be back. Birds have to keep their eggs warm while the chicks are growing inside."

Wilma's dad went on, "Later on the female will sit on the eggs all the time, until they hatch."

"But what are we going to do about mending the old shed?" asked Wilma.

"Well, we just won't be able to until after the eggs are hatched and the chicks have grown big enough to fly away."

"But that will be ages," said Wilma. "Can't we move the nest somewhere else where the robins won't be disturbed?"

"Oh no," said Wilma's dad. "If we do that, the robins will never go back to their nest again. The eggs will go cold and the little chicks inside will die."

"What shall we do, then?" cried Wilma.

Her dad said, "We'll have to leave the shed just as it is. We won't come anywhere near it. There will be time enough to mend it after the birds have grown up and gone away."

And that's just what they did.

Of course, Wilma's dad couldn't get his garden tools, or the lawn-mower. Wilf and Wilma couldn't get out their go-kart.

Stage 2

But Wilma's dad went to his neighbour and said, "Will you lend me your lawn-mower? I've got robins nesting on mine!" And the neighbour said, "Of course I will. I hope all those little robins hatch out safely."

Wilf and Wilma went to see Biff and Chip. They said, "May we ride on your go-kart? We've got robins nesting on ours!"

Biff and Chip said, "Of course you can. After all, you mustn't disturb the nesting birds."

In time there were five little chicks in the nest. You can guess how busy the robins were then, with five young chicks to feed.

"I'm afraid the robins won't be able to nest there next year," said Wilma's dad. "It was nice having them, but I've decided to buy a new shed after all."

Ask the children

- How do birds keep their eggs warm?
- What would happen to the chicks inside the eggs if they weren't kept warm?
- What would happen if they moved the nest or disturbed it?
- Can you think of other ways of respecting and caring for living creatures?

Cross-curricular link

Knowledge & understanding of the world: / Science: make observations of common objects and communicate these
- What materials has the bird used to make their nest?
- Why do you think the bird chose the shed?

Stage 3

21 Anneena

Before reading
Show Card 21 to the children and write **Anneena** at the top of the card.

Read to the children
Biff and Chip have two other friends. They are called Anneena and Nadim. They are both in the same class as Biff and Chip. Nadim and Anneena are not brother and sister. They live in different streets to each other. They don't live as close to Biff and Chip as Wilf and Wilma so they don't play with them as often.

This is what Biff said about Anneena. "If ever I wanted anyone to help me, I'd ask Anneena." That's because Anneena is always kind to everyone. Anneena is good with her hands and likes making things. Biff always tries to sit next to Anneena because she knows that Anneena has lots of good ideas.

This is what Wilf said about Anneena. "One day, Anneena will be either a famous badmington player or a runner."

Wilf said that because it's hard to beat Anneena at any sport. She's good with a bat and a ball and she can run really fast. Anneena can run faster than Wilf and she's much better than him at badmington.

Ask the children
- Why does Biff like Anneena?
- What are the things Anneena is good at?
- What does Wilf think Anneena will grow up to be?
- What is Anneena doing in this picture?

Cross-curricular links
PSHE / RE: understand different needs, views, cultures and beliefs
- What is Anneena wearing?
- How do her clothes differ from your clothes?
- Why do you think she is wearing those clothes?

22 Nadim

Before reading
Show Card 22 to the children and write **Nadim** at the top of the card.

 ### Read to the children
This is Nadim. He is seven years old, just like Biff and Chip. You say his name like this: Na–deem. Nadim loves telling jokes and he likes making everyone laugh. Sometimes his teacher has to say, "Nadim, it's time to stop telling jokes and get on with your work quietly."
   Nadim loves reading and he enjoys doing numbers, Chip likes sitting next to him because Nadim will help Chip when he gets stuck!
   But what Nadim loves most of all is his computer. He loves playing computer games and he's really good at them. In fact the only person who can beat him is Wilma – and that's only sometimes.
This is one of Nadim's jokes:
Q: Why did the banana go to the doctor?
A: Because it wasn't peeling very well.

Ask the children
- How old is Nadim?
- What else does Nadim like to do as well as reading and number?
- What is your favourite subject at school?
- What other things do you like to do?

◀▶ Cross-curricular links
Knowledge & understanding of the world / ICT: identify the uses of everyday technology
- What other things in the room can Nadim use with his computer?
- What things at home do you have that use a computer?
- How do computers help us?

Stage 3

23 Nadim's Birthday Treat

Before reading

Show Card 23 to the children and ask what they think is happening in the picture. Then tell the story.

 ## Read to the children

It was Nadim's birthday. Nadim's dad came round and said, "We are going to have a party on the beach. Would Biff, Chip, and Kipper like to come along?"

"Oh yes!" said Biff, Chip, and Kipper. "You bet we would."

On Saturday afternoon, Nadim's dad called for them in a minibus. The minibus was full of children. There were only three seats left for Biff, Chip, and Kipper.

"You deserve a medal, taking all these children to the beach," said Biff and Chip's mum.

"The more the merrier," said Nadim's dad, and the minibus set off.

It was quite a long drive to the beach. As they were driving along the minibus began to puff out great clouds of black smoke. Nadim's dad looked worried. "I think we're going to break down," he said.

The engine began to cough and splutter. "Pull in to that car park ahead," said Nadim's mum, "before we break down altogether." And just as she said this, the engine went "clatter, rattle, chug, chug", and stopped.

"We've still got enough speed to run into the car park," said Nadim's dad.

He got out when the minibus had stopped and took a look at the engine. Just as he did great drops of rain began to fall.

"Now what are we going to do?" said Nadim's mum. "Here we are in a minibus, miles from anywhere with lots of children, and it's going to pour with rain."

"When are we going to get to the beach?" asked Nadim. "It's getting stuffy in this minibus."

At that moment, an enormous truck drove into the car park. It was very tall and very long.

"It's a wonder he can get that thing round corners," said Chip.

Nadim's dad said, "I'll go and see if the driver can give me a lift to a garage to get help." And he got out of the minibus.

A few minutes later, the driver of the enormous truck came over to the minibus. He was a big man with a big round smiling face.

"I've got a radio in my truck so I've called for help to fix your minibus." He smiled at all the children. "And I've got a surprise for you lot," he said.

He went over and opened the huge back doors of his enormous truck. And do you know what was inside? Nothing! There was nothing in it at all. It was like an enormous, great big empty room. "Come on," called the man. "You can have your picnic in here. Run across, and don't get wet as you go."

◀▶ Cross-curricular links

Mathematical development / Numeracy: use everyday words to describe position, direction and movement
- Where are the children sitting? (in the van)
- What would happen if were sitting on the van, or beside the van?

24 The Party in the Truck

Before reading
Show Card 24 to the children and continue the story.

 Read to the children

It was very clean inside the enormous truck. There was a light on the ceiling. There was a big ledge at one end for Nadim's mum to set out all the food for the picnic. And there was plenty of room to play party games.

The big truck driver with the smiley face did some conjuring tricks.

"I'm going to be a truck driver, when I grow up," whispered Chip.

Stage 3

At last Nadim's dad came in and said, "It's stopped raining and the men from the garage have come with a breakdown lorry. They said they can fix the minibus here in the car park."

There wasn't time to go to the beach after that. It was time to go home. But everyone agreed that it had been a fantastic birthday party in the back of the truck.

"I can't wait to tell everyone about it at school on Monday," said Wilf.

"When I grow up," said Kipper, "I'm going to live in a truck like this. I'm not going to live in a house."

Everyone laughed.

Ask the children

- Where was Nadim hoping to go in the minibus for his birthday treat?
- Where did Nadim eventually have his birthday party?
- Why was it a good birthday party after all?
- How do you feel when you are disappointed?

Cross-curricular links

Personal, social and emotional development: taking turns and sharing fairly

PHSE: the need for agreed values and codes of behaviour for groups of people

- What games are they playing at the party?
- Whose turn is it for the game?
- Why do you have to take it in turns?
- What would happen if you didn't take turns?

Stage 4

25 A Bird's-eye View

Before reading
Show Card 25 to the children and write **The Neighbourhood** in the space at the top of the card.

📖 Read to the children
Have you ever wondered what a bird sees when it is flying up in the sky? Well, that is a bird's-eye view. This bird's-eye view shows the neighbourhood where Biff, Chip and Kipper live, play and go to school with all their friends. It shows the road with the house where Biff, Chip and Kipper live in all the early stories, and it shows the big old house that they will move to in Stage 4. It shows the house where Wilf and Wilma live, part of the park with the play area, the stream with the wooden bridge, and the school. Biff, Chip and Kipper have lots of exciting adventures in the neighbourhood with their family and friends, and we will all be reading about all these places in the story books.

Ask the children
- If you were a bird what could you see if you were up in the sky above the neighbourhood?
- Where is Biff, Chip and Kipper's house? Point to the swing in their garden.
- Where do Wilf and Wilma live? Point to the shed in their back garden.
- Where is the park, the stream with the wooden bridge and the rope swing?
- Can you see the big old house with the tree house in the garden?
- Can you see Biff and Chip's classroom?

◀▶ Cross-curricular links
Knowledge & understanding of the world: identify features in the place where they live
Geography: be able to annotate a simple map
- How is this area the same or different from your local area?
- Can you see a house that looks similar to your house?

Oxford Reading Tree resources

There is a range of material available at Stages 1, 1+, 2, 3 and 4.

Teacher support
- Teacher's Handbook
- Storybooks with Teacher's Notes
- Take-Home Cards for each story
- Guided Reading Cards for core stories at Stage 1 First Words, Stage 1+ First Sentences, Stage 2, 3 and 4.
- Extended Stories
- Workbooks
- Storytapes
- Sequencing Cards Photocopy Masters
- Oxford Reading Tree Games Stages 1–3
- Group Activity Sheets Book 1 Stages 1–3
- Fact Finders Topic Starters
- My Word Book
- Rubber Stamps

Further reading
- Branch Library

Electronic
- First Story Rhymes CD-Rom
- Clip Art CD-Rom
- Talking Stories CD-Rom
- Floppy and Friends CD-Rom
- Oxford Reading Tree Online www.OxfordReadingTree.com

For developing further awareness
- Alphaber Frieze, Tabletop Alphabet Mats, Alphabet Photocpy Masters
- Card Games

OXFORD
UNIVERSITY PRESS

Great Clarendon Street, Oxford OX2 6DP

Oxford University Press is a department of the University of Oxford. It furthers the University's objective of excellence in research, scholarship, and education by publishing worldwide in

Oxford New York

Auckland Bangkok Buenos Aires Cape Town Chennai
Dar es Salaam Delhi Hong Kong Istanbul Karachi Kolkata
Kuala Lumpur Madrid Melbourne Mexico City Mumbai Nairobi
São Paulo Shanghai Taipei Tokyo Toronto

Oxford is a registered trade mark of Oxford University Press in the UK and in certain other countries

© Oxford University Press 2004

First published 2004

The moral rights of the author have been asserted

Database right Oxford University Press (maker)

All rights reserved. No part of this publication may be reproduced, stored in a retrieval system, or transmitted, in any form or by any means, without the prior permission in writing of Oxford University Press, or as expressly permitted by law, or under terms agreed with the appropriate reprographics rights organization. Enquiries concerning reproduction outside the scope of the above should be sent to the Rights Department, Oxford University Press, at the address above

You must not circulate this book in any other binding or cover and you must impose this same condition on any acquirer

British Library Cataloguing in Publication Data

Data available

Cover illustration Alex Brychta

Teacher's Notes: ISBN 0 19 845334 5

10 9 8 7 6 5 4 3 2

Page make-up by IFA Design Ltd, Plymouth, Devon

Printed in China